to Sew

Sewing Room Accessories

Dedication

As this book is full of projects for people who sew, I'm dedicating
it to you all! Those who have been sewing for a lifetime, those
who have just started and those who are inspired. I hope you
enjoy sewing and sharing every project you make!

Love to Sew

Debbie Shore

Sewing Room Accessories

Search Press

First published in 2017

Search Press Limited
Wellwood, North Farm Road,
Tunbridge Wells, Kent TN2 3DR

Text copyright © Debbie Shore 2017

Photographs © Garie Hind

Styling and modelling by Kimberley Hind

Design copyright © Search Press Ltd. 2017

ISBN: 978-1-78221-335-2

The Publishers and author can accept no
responsibility for any consequences arising
from the information, advice or instructions
given in this publication.

Suppliers
If you have difficulty in obtaining any of the
materials and equipment mentioned in this
book, then please visit the Search Press
website for details of suppliers:
www.searchpress.com

Printed in China

Pumpkin Pincushion, page 16

Ribbon Stash, page 20

Tidy Caddy, page 28

Seam Press, page 44

Ironing Station, page 46

Sewing Case, page 22

Machine Cover and Mat, page 26

Contents

Cutting Mat Carrier, page 32

Sewing Circle, page 34

Tool Roll, page 36

Chair Storage, page 40

Sewing Machine Cover, page 50

Pin and Pattern Pouch, page 54

Sewing Book Cover, page 56

Carry Case, page 60

Introduction

Making your sewing area pretty as well as practical is a way of creating an inviting place to work and, of course, if you make your own accessories you can easily co-ordinate your fabrics to match your home decor. This book contains lovely, useful projects that I hope you will enjoy making, whether they be my plump little pumpkin pincushion (see page 16) or my practical tool roll (see page 36), which is just packed with handy pockets. After all, you can never have enough storage space. The sides of an armchair and the back of a door are usually wasted spaces – so why not create pockets and pouches to make the most of your space and help to keep yourself organised?

But as well as storage, I have also included some tried-and-tested projects that will help you out while you are sewing. Pressing is as important as sewing – my handy seam press (see page 44) can be made to any size you like depending on the kind of projects you're making, while a small pressing station next to your sewing machine is invaluable (see page 46).

Many of us also have like-minded friends who just love to sew, and I'd like to think that this book is filled with gift ideas that you can make for them. A word of warning: you may find yourself spending more time sewing than ever before!

I've mostly used quilting cotton for my projects; if you have a fine fabric, a little spray of starch adds stiffness, or you can back your fabric with interfacing if you need to. I've used a 5mm (¼in) seam allowance unless otherwise stated.

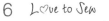

Materials & equipment

Fabrics

I prefer to use 100% cotton quilting fabrics, available in such a wide range of prints and colours. Small prints are useful for small projects or appliqué, as you don't lose the pattern when you cut. Choose prints that complement each other and a few solid colours to break up the busyness of patterns.

Choose a good-quality cotton and there will be less shrinkage. I don't usually pre-wash fabric that will end up being a project that can be spot cleaned, like my sewing machine dust cover (page 50), but if an item will be washed, for instance if used in the kitchen, it is always a good idea to pre-wash to avoid disappointment later.

Wadding/batting

This is positioned between outer and lining fabrics to give them form and stability. Choose a fusible wadding/batting – also known as fusible fleece – that is ironed onto the back of your fabric. If you can't find this, use a sew-in wadding/batting and spray on repositionable fabric adhesive to hold it in place while sewing. Synthetic types are available – including those made from recycled plastic bottles! – but I prefer natural types, which are made from cotton, wool, bamboo or soya, and tend to be softer and more breathable than synthetic. I tend not to pre-wash wadding/batting, but you should always follow the manufacturer's instructions.

Also available on the market is a thermal, heat-resistant wadding/batting, which I have used for the ironing board cover (see page 46). For this project you will need heat-reflective fabric as well as wadding/batting – I used a piece of ironing-board cover, which has the same effect. The new kid on the block is foam stabiliser or fusible foam, which adds a real firmness to your project but is easy to sew through. It is perfect if you want the item to stand up and keep its shape (see the sewing machine cover on page 50).

Threads

Always use good-quality thread – your project will last longer and the seams will be stronger. Good-quality thread feels smoother than poor-quality types, and will leave less lint inside your sewing machine. Try to use cotton thread with cotton fabric, and the same thread in the top and bottom of your machine.

For hand sewing, use a stronger thread that can withstand pulling. Silk thread for appliqué gives a luxurious look and feel to your projects.

Sewing machine

There are many sewing machines on the market nowadays, with varied features and prices. If you are buying for the first time, I suggest a computerised machine. Although they usually cost more than a simple electronic machine, they are generally easier to use. Look for a needle up/down option, as this makes it easy to pivot around corners, and if you want to do free-motion embroidery, you will need a drop feed dog facility. For the projects in this book, you will need a straight stitch and an adjustable zigzag. You will also need a free-motion or darning foot. On the whole, the more stitches and features, the more costly the machine, so think carefully about where your sewing journey will take you, and shop wisely.

Other materials

I try to keep materials to a minimum, as we're all on a budget, but here are a few things that will make your sewing easier and your cutting accurate.

Bamboo creaser: this is a handy little tool used to push out corners without tearing your fabric. It can also be used to crease small lengths of fabric instead of ironing them.

Tacking glue pen: try gluing instead of tacking/basting to save time. The correct glues will wash out of your fabric, so make sure you choose one that is designed for the purpose. These temporary glues are useful for holding zips in place as you sew on your machine, and are commonly used with English paper piecing.

Erasable fabric pens: some inks are designed to disappear after a period of time: these are air-erasable pens. Some inks are removed when wet – known as water-soluble pens. I prefer heat-erasable ink pens – the ink disappears with friction or the heat from an iron. Be aware that the ink from water-soluble and air-erasable pens becomes permanent if ironed.

Pinking shears: these scissors can give a decorative edge to fabrics such as felt, and can help to prevent woven fabrics fraying. In effect, they cut the fabric at tiny 45-degree angles, or bias cuts, which don't allow the fabric to fray. They are also useful for trimming curved seams to help the stitch line sit flat.

Fabric clips: these are really useful when your fabric is too thick to pin, or if you're using materials such as oilcloth, as pins would leave holes in the fabric surface.

Bodkin: although you can use a safety pin to thread ribbon or cord through drawstring channels, occasionally they will come undone and sometimes they can tear your ribbon. A good alternative is a bodkin, which is a bit like a large-eyed blunt needle. Thread it with your ribbon or cord before feeding it through the drawstring channel.

Bias tape maker: if you're making your own bias binding, thread your strips of fabric through this handy tool and it will be folded to the centre. As you pull the tape through, press with your iron to set the creases. They're available in a range of sizes – 2.5cm (1in) is the one I use most.

Basic techniques

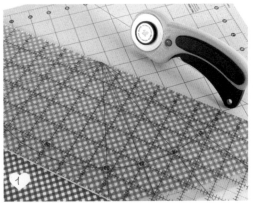

Creating bias strips

Although bias strips (also referred to as bias binding and bias tape) can be bought in many colours and sizes, I like to make my own, as this is cost-effective and means I can coordinate it with my fabrics.

Bias binding is a strip of fabric cut on the diagonal, at a 45-degree angle, which allows a little 'give' so that the fabric stretches around curves without puckering. To cut your fabric accurately, you will need a rotary cutter, rectangular ruler and cutting mat.

1 Lay your fabric squarely on the cutting mat, and place the 45-degree mark on your ruler on the straight edge of the fabric. Cut along the ruler.

2 Turn your fabric over and use the straight side of the ruler to measure the width you need. For 2.5cm (1in) bias binding, you need to cut 5cm (2in) of fabric. As you are cutting the strips, the fabric will stretch, so fold it in half diagonally and cut through two, three or four layers at a time.

3 To join the strips, lay two pieces right sides together, overlapping at right angles. Draw a diagonal line from one corner to the other, as in the photograph. Pin, then sew along this line. Trim the raw edge back to around 3mm (1/8in) and press the seam open.

4 To make bias binding, you need to fold both of the long edges of the tape into the centre and press. The easiest way to do this is to use either a bias binding machine or a small bias tape maker. As you pull the strip through this, it folds it in two – press with your iron to fix the folds. If you don't have a tape maker, carefully fold both long edges to the centre of the fabric strip and press. Be careful not to get your fingers too close to the iron!

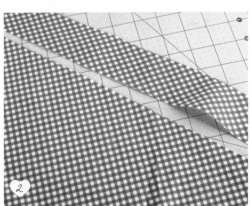

Applying bias binding

Bias binding is one of those products I use such a lot of, whether shop-bought or homemade. It gives such a neat edge, not only to quilts, but to oven gloves, table mats, handbags and more! A neat, mitred corner really gives a professional finish to a project like my sewing machine mat, and it's not difficult when you know how...

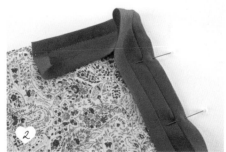

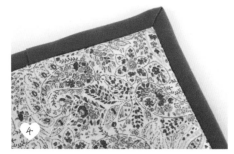

1 Open out the bias tape and place right sides together with the edge of your project. Fold in the first end of the binding, as shown. Sew along the crease line but stop 1cm (½in) from the corner and back-tack to stop the stitches coming undone.

2 Take the tape along the second side, making a triangular pleat in the corner. Fold the pleat away from your stitch line, pin in place, and sew along the second side, again stopping 1cm (½in) from the end.

3 Continue in the same way around the next three corners, and when you're back to where you started, overlap the ends of the tape by about 5mm (¼in).

4 Fold the tape over to the back, tucking the folded edge under and you should see neat mitres forming: mirror the same mitres on the reverse. I like to use fabric clips to hold the edge as the fabric is now quite thick for pinning.

5 Sew the bias tape in place by hand with a slip stitch, making sure your machine stitch line is covered by the tape.

6 When you're finished, you'll have really neat, square corners both from the front of your work...

7 ... and from the back!

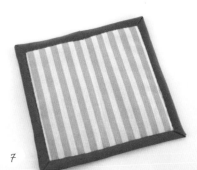

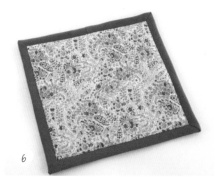

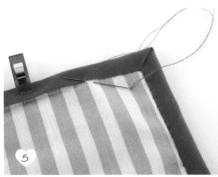

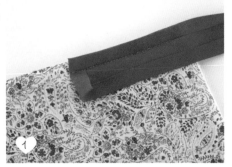

How to draw the perfect heart

The perfect heart can be quite a tricky shape to draw, so here's my foolproof method:

1 Fold a piece of card in half. Take a small plate, ribbon spool or anything round of the size you want, and place it over the fold.

2 Draw around the curve.

3 Take a ruler, and draw a line from the side of the circle to the fold. If you make a short line, you'll have a fat heart, a longer line will give you a 'Scandinavian-style' heart – simple!

Appliqué

Appliqué is the method of applying a decorative fabric motif to your work. This could be a hand-stitched felt shape, as with the heart embellishment on my sewing case, or shapes cut from pre-printed fabric like the houses on my sewing machine cover and mat, which I chose to sew down using free-motion embroidery.

To make the application easier, use a repositionable spray fabric adhesive to keep the shapes in place, or iron a sheet of fusible adhesive to the back of the fabric before cutting. Then peel off the paper backing and re-iron the designs into position.

Satin stitch

If you are machine sewing, form a dense line by shortening your zigzag stitch to make it into a satin stitch. This technique will also help prevent woven fabrics from fraying.

Blanket stitch

Felt or fabric appliqué looks charming when hand embroidered with blanket or running stitch. Try hand stitching in blanket stitch around woven fabrics too – this gives a rustic look to your work. For a neater look, use the blanket or pin stitch on your sewing machine.

Blind hem stitch

Try your machine's blind hem stitch if you don't want to see so much of the stitch. Always test out the stitch you would like to use on scrap fabric first, to make sure you are happy with it.

Free-motion embroidery

I think this is the easiest way to sew on appliqué pieces as you don't have to be too accurate or even sew in a straight line! Use a free-motion embroidery foot (sometimes called a 'darning foot') on your sewing machine and drop the feed dogs. Then move the fabric under the needle in any direction you like, a bit like drawing with thread. To make it a little easier, draw your stitch line first with an erasable fabric pen.

Machine stitching

1 Blanket/pin stitch

Most sewing machines will have a blanket stitch; more advanced machines may have a few variations. I like this stitch to edge appliqué; it gives a rustic, hand-finished look to your work. See the heart appliqué on my sewing case on page 22.

2 Satin stitch

This is your zigzag stitch, with the stitch length at its shortest to create a solid line. It's ideal for edging and appliqué as the stitches are so tight your fabric won't fray. If you take the needle slightly over the edge of your fabric, the stitch will wrap around and finish a raw edge off perfectly, as with my envelope case on page 20.

3 Straight stitch

This is the stitch you'll use most, for sewing seams and edge stitching. Edge stitching is a top-stitch sewn close to the edge of your work: it gives a professional, crisp look to your projects, as with the sewing case on page 22.

4 Zigzag stitch

This can be used decoratively, but is also a useful stitch to help stop seams from fraying, particularly on items that will be washed.

5 Decorative stitches

These will vary from machine to machine: some are very simple and others quite ornate. Try embroidering a strip of plain ribbon to add interest, or use instead of an edge stitch. If you have the time and patience, you could stitch a whole piece of fabric with rows of different stitches to create your own unique design!

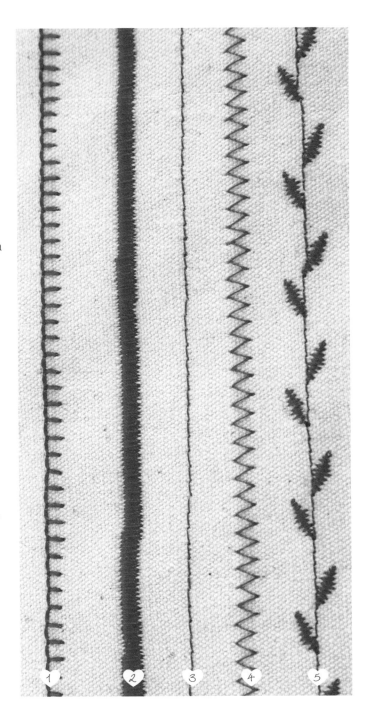

Pumpkin Pincushion

This decorative pincushion is actually a really practical shape. I like a pincushion I can use without taking my eyes off my work, that has space to store not just my pins, but needles, machine needles and safety pins, and that doesn't roll around my sewing table!

Materials

- 2 circles of fabric measuring 13cm (5in) across
- 2 circles of fabric measuring 15cm (6in) across
- about 75g (2¾oz) of toy filling
- embroidery thread
- 50cm (½yd) of 4cm (1½in) wide lace
- 50cm (½yd) of 1cm (½in) wide ribbon
- 10cm (4in) string of beads
- 1 button

Tools

- sewing machine and thread
- fabric scissors
- pinking shears (optional)
- iron
- embroidery needle for hand sewing
- a long needle – mine measures 13cm (5in)
- rectangular ruler
- erasable fabric pen

1 Take one large and one small circle – these will be the top of the bottom section and the bottom of the top section – and cut a slit in the centre of each, 5cm (2in) long. Hand or machine sew over the ends of each cut to stop them ripping when you come to stuff the pincushion. If you have a bar tack stitch on your machine, this is perfect!

2 Take the large cut circle from step 1, and the uncut small circle. On the right side, divide each into 6 segments using an erasable pen and the 60-degree line on your ruler.

3 Sew the large and small circles right sides together in pairs, then snip all the way round with pinking shears. If you don't have any pinking shears, make small 'v' shaped cuts into the seam allowance, avoiding the stitches. This will help the seam to sit flat.

4 Turn each circle right side out through the slit you made in the centre.

5 Stuff each piece tightly with toy filling, then over-sew the openings closed by hand. Don't worry about being too neat here – you won't see the stitches when the pincushion is put together.

6 Take a piece of embroidery thread, about 76cm (30in) long, thread your long needle and tie a large knot about 10cm (4in) from the end. Push your needle down through the centre of one of the circles, bring it up following one of the lines you've marked, and take it back through the centre. Pull tight and repeat until you have divided your six segments. Tie the two ends of the thread, knot them and trim the ends, then do the same with the second stuffed piece to create your two 'pumpkins'.

7 Using a length of embroidery thread and your embroidery needle, take running stitches through one long edge of the lace to gather it. Leave the ends loose to make tying easier.

8 Gather a 30cm (12in) length of ribbon in the same way, but this time pull together and tie to make a little rosette (see finished piece, right, for reference).

9 Place the small pumpkin on top of the large one with the slitted sides meeting in the centre, and with embroidery thread and your long needle, sew straight through the centre of both. Take the needle and thread through the button on the bottom of the pincushion, back through the other hole in the button, through the pumpkins...

10 ...and through the rosette on the top. Tie the thread off to secure it.

11 Tie the gathered lace around the middle of the pincushion and knot. Make a bow from the remaining ribbon and sew to one side, along with the string of beads.

Ribbon Stash

Stop ribbons and bias binding getting tangled up with this simple storage idea that you can also use to save buttons. Put the cards in your sewing case (see page 22) or use the coordinating envelope case.

Materials

- 8 pieces of card measuring 7.5 x 5cm (3 x 2in) – 2 for each finished card
- 8 pieces of plain fabric measuring 10 x 7.5cm (4 x 3in) – 2 for each finished card
- lace, ribbon, bias binding or cord to store on your cards, or buttons if desired
- decorative pins
- for the envelope, 2 pieces of fabric measuring 18cm (7in) square
- 1 magnetic fastener
- 1 button to decorate

Tools

- sewing machine, thread and denim needle (optional)
- fabric scissors
- hand-sewing needle
- iron
- spray fabric adhesive
- strong fabric glue
- fabric clips (optional)

1 Wrap a piece of fabric around each card, with the right side facing out; fold over the edges and glue in place. Trim away the folded corners, but don't cut right into the corner as the fabric may fray.

2 Glue the panels together in pairs, raw sides together.

3 Hand sew around all four sides with a whip stitch – you could machine stitch instead, but you'll need to pop a denim needle onto your machine, as it's a stronger needle required for sewing through card.

4 Wrap the ribbon, binding, cord or lace around the centre of each card, and secure with a decorative pin.

5 If you wish to use a card for buttons, hand sew them on.

6 To make a fabric envelope for storing your cards, take the two squares of fabric and adhere them wrong sides together with spray adhesive. Sew around all four edges with satin stitch on your machine, taking the needle slightly over the edge of the layers of fabric to wrap the thread over. If you have any gaps when you've finished, simply sew around a second time.

7 Fold in half twice to mark the centre of the square, then unfold. Fold two opposite corners inwards, overlapping by 1cm (½in); press.

8 Fold the bottom of the envelope to the centre, press, and add one half of the magnetic clasp just inside the point, as shown on the facing page. Glue the folded fabric with strong fabric glue. Use clips to hold together if you wish.

9 Attach the second half of the magnetic clasp to the lining side of the opposite point of the envelope, then add the button to the right side to hide the back of the fastener.

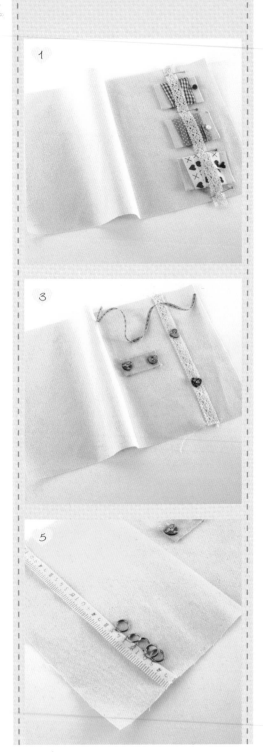

Sewing Case

Every household needs a sewing kit for maintenance and repairs, and you can adapt the contents of this booklet for a beginner or experienced sewer. You'll always know where to find a needle and thread, safety pins, scissors and spare buttons!

Materials

- the four hand-made storage cards from pages 20–21
- 1 piece of plain lining fabric measuring 38 x 25.5cm (15 x 10in) – I've used a heavyweight calico/muslin
- 1 piece of fusible fleece measuring 38 x 25.5cm (15 x 10in)
- 1 piece of outer fabric measuring 38 x 25.5cm (15 x 10in)
- 28cm (11in) length of 2.5cm (1in) wide lace to hold the storage cards
- 5 buttons
- fabric heart measuring 11.5 x 15cm (4½ x 6in), see page 14
- 2 ribbons to tie, each measuring 20 x 1cm (8 x ½in)
- for the scissor holder, 7.5cm (3in) length of 4cm (1½in) wide ribbon
- 35.5cm (14in) length of 5mm (¼in) wide ribbon
- for the embroidery-thread organiser, 25.5cm (10in) of 1cm (½in) wide ribbon
- for the pincushion, a 7.5cm (3in) card circle to use as a template
- a circle of fabric measuring 13cm (5in) across
- a small amount of toy filling
- 5 metal rings, 1cm (½in) across

Tools

- sewing machine and thread
- iron
- fabric scissors
- craft scissors
- embroidery needle for hand stitching

1 Take the lining piece of fabric, fold in half widthways and crease to mark the centre. Place three of the storage cards in a row down one side of the right-hand 'page', 7.5cm (3in) from the edge, and lay the 28cm (11in) strip of lace over the top. Pin at each end of the lace and in between the cards – don't pull the lace too tightly or they will be difficult to remove.

2 Tack/baste each end of the lace to secure to the lining, and sew a button in between each card.

3 For the scissor holder, take the 7.5cm (3in) length of 4cm (1½in) wide ribbon and fold the ends under twice to prevent fraying. Pin to the left of the storage cards, making sure they don't overlap, then sew a button through each end of the ribbon to secure it to the lining. To hold the scissors in place, sew the centre of the 35.5cm (14in) strip of narrow ribbon 4cm (1½in) above the wide ribbon. This ribbon will tie a bow through the scissors' handles.

4 Now for the embroidery-thread holder. Sew the metal rings by hand to the right-hand edge of the 25.5cm (10in) ribbon, in a row, starting 5cm (2in) from the bottom.

5 Sew the ribbon in place at each end, positioning it 6.5cm (2½in) from the left-hand edge of the lining.

6 To make the pincushion, place the circle of card on the back of the 13cm (5in) circle of fabric, and use running stitch to gather and secure the edge; press.

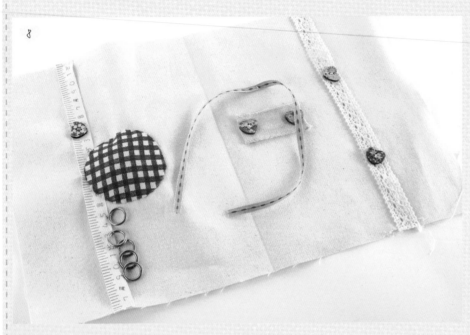

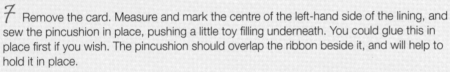

7 Remove the card. Measure and mark the centre of the left-hand side of the lining, and sew the pincushion in place, pushing a little toy filling underneath. You could glue this in place first if you wish. The pincushion should overlap the ribbon beside it, and will help to hold it in place.

8 Pop the remaining storage card underneath the ribbon above the pincushion, and sew on the remaining button to make a holder for it.

9 Fold the outer fabric in half to mark the centre. Pin the fabric heart to the right-hand side of the cover, and blanket stitch all the way around, removing the pins as you go. Iron the fusible fleece to the back of the outer cover fabric.

10 Take the ribbon ties and sew, facing inwards, to the centre of each side of the cover, as shown right.

11 Pin the cover and linings right sides together and sew all the way round, leaving a gap of about 10cm (4in) in one side for turning through.

12 Turn right side out and press. Edge stitch all the way round. Fold the whole case in half and crease the centre, then sew along this crease line.

13 Fill with your storage cards, thread, scissors and pins.

13

Machine Cover and Mat

A sewing machine mat will help to reduce noise and protect your table from scratches. My mat doubles up as a dust cover by draping over the machine and tying at the sides. The little village scene is so much fun to sew, and of course you could add trees, flowers and pathways to make your mat unique! I enjoy free-motion embroidery, but use a satin stitch to edge the pieces if you prefer.

Materials

Measure the width of your machine and add 5cm (2in), then measure from the front to the back, over the top of the machine and again add 5cm (2in). My measurements are 48 x 74cm (19 x 29in) so that's what I'm basing this project on. Adapt the size to suit.

- ♥ 2 pieces of plain fabric measuring 48 x 74cm (19 x 29in)
- ♥ 1 piece of wadding/batting or single-sided fusible fleece measuring 48 x 74cm (19 x 29in)
- ♥ 1 piece of tear-away stabiliser measuring 48 x 35.5cm (19 x 14in)
- ♥ 1 semicircle of fabric measuring 30cm (12in) across (large hill)
- ♥ 1 semicircle of fabric measuring 20cm (8in) across (small hill)
- ♥ 3 rectangles of fabric measuring 7.5 x 10cm (3 x 4in) for the houses – don't worry about these being perfect in size, it's quite nice when the houses look a little quirky!

- ♥ 3 triangles of fabric measuring 9cm (3½in) on each side for the roofs
- ♥ 3 rectangles of fabric measuring 2.5 x 1cm (1 x ½in) for the chimneys
- ♥ 3 squares of plain fabric measuring 5 x 5cm (2 x 2in) for the windows
- ♥ 76cm (30in) of 1cm (½in) wide lace for the fences – I've used 40.5cm (16in) of dark and 35.5cm (14in) of light-coloured lace
- ♥ 4 lengths of 1cm (½in) wide ribbon each measuring 30cm (12in) long for ties
- ♥ 254cm (100in) bias binding

Tools

- ♥ sewing machine, thread and free-motion foot
- ♥ fabric scissors
- ♥ heat-erasable fabric pen
- ♥ iron
- ♥ repositionable spray fabric adhesive

1 Fuse the fleece to the back of one of your large plain pieces of fabric. If you're using standard wadding/batting, adhere with repositionable spray fabric adhesive. Drape the fabric over your machine, and crease across the fabric at the top front of the machine to mark your appliqué area.

2 Arrange the cottage and hill pieces on the front of the cover – at this point you can see if you'd like to add any more pieces. Check that the lace for the fences looks good. Place the stabiliser behind the appliquéd area – this will help when embroidering.

3   Starting with the large hill, curve a strip of lace underneath the dome and adhere both hill and lace in place with spray adhesive; free-motion embroider three or four times around the curve. Save a little lace by not placing it where the second hill will go.

4   Sew on the small hill in the same way, then add the houses, windows, then finally the roofs and chimneys. Using erasable pen, draw a line of smoke from one of the chimneys, swirling across the cover and stitch over the top.

5   On each long side, measure 18cm (7in) from each corner and mark. Sew a strip of ribbon, facing inwards, to each mark.

6   Place the whole cover, wrong sides together with the plain backing fabric and adhere with repositionable spray. Apply bias binding around all four sides, mitring the corners (see page 13).

7   With the ties done up you have a padded cover to place over your machine; undo the ties and you have a mat for it to sit on!

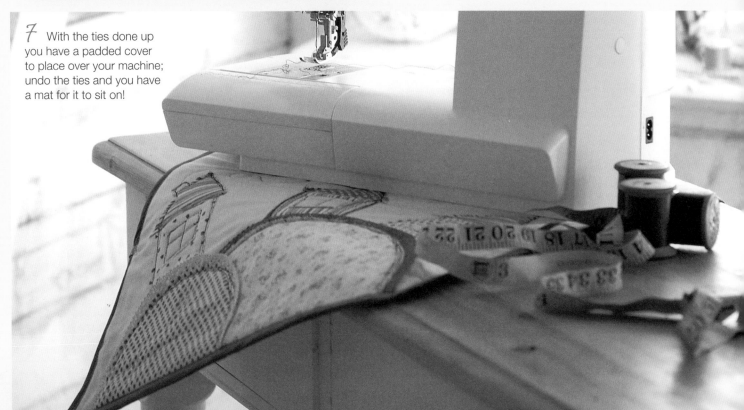

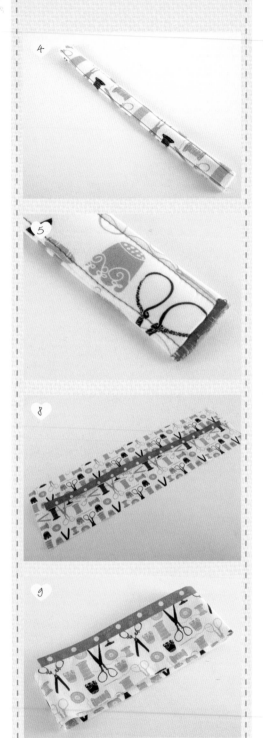

Tidy Caddy

Keep your sewing area tidy with this bucket-shaped caddy, with eight useful pockets to store your most-used items.

Materials

- 23cm (¼yd) fabric A (mine is the spot)
- 90cm (1yd) fabric B (mine is the sewing notions)
- 89 x 25.5cm (35 x 10in) fusible fleece
- 70cm (27in) of 1cm (½in) wide ribbon
- 10 buttons – follow the manufacturer's instructions if you want fabric-covered buttons like mine
- embroidery thread

Tools

- sewing machine and thread
- fabric scissors
- embroidery needle for hand sewing
- iron
- erasable fabric pen
- ruler
- safety pin or bodkin

1 Cut two circles of fabric A for the base, each measuring 20cm (8in) across. Fuse fleece to the wrong side of one piece.

2 For the sides, cut two pieces of fabric A measuring 63.5 x 20cm (25 x 8in), and again, fuse fleece to the wrong side of one piece.

3 Cut two strips of fabric B measuring 158 x 15cm (62 x 6in) for the pockets – you may have to join two pieces together.

4 Cut one piece of fabric B measuring 20 x 10cm (8 x 4in) for the handle; fuse fleece to the wrong side. Fold the long sides to the centre, then fold in half. Top-stitch along both sides.

5 Satin stitch across the two ends of the handle.

6 Cut two pieces of fabric B, each measuring 63.5 x 10cm (25 x 4in), and one strip of fabric A measuring 66 x 5cm (26 x 2in) for the drawstring section. Fold the ends of fabric A over twice and sew.

7 Fold the strip of fabric A in half lengthways, wrong sides together and press. Place the fabric B drawstring section pieces right sides together, and sandwich the folded strip of fabric A in between, with the raw edges together at the top. The folded section should be 1cm (½in) shorter at each end than the fabric B pieces.

8 Sew the three sections together across the top. Open out and press.

9 Fold the whole piece right sides together so that the short sides meet. Sew along the short end. Push one side inside the other so that the drawstring channel is at the top and press again.

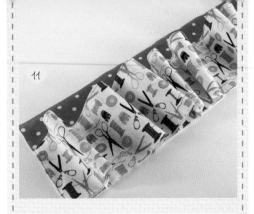

10 Take the two pocket pieces and sew them together across the top long edge, right sides together. Fold over so that they sit with the wrong sides together and press. Edge stitch 3mm ($^1/_8$in) from the top.

11 Fold the pocket fabric in half and crease the centre line, fold in half again and crease the quarters, then in half again and crease the eighths. Open out the fabric and mark these lines with erasable fabric pen. You could measure and mark the fabric into eighths if you find that easier. Mark the side section of fabric A that you've backed with fleece in the same way. Place the pocket strip over the top of the side piece, tack/baste the sides together, then pin at the marked lines. You'll see the eight pocket shapes starting to form. Stitch 5mm (¼in) in from each side.

12 Stitch along each of the marked lines to divide. Remove the pins. Flatten each pocket shape and re-pin so that the folds meet – leave 1cm (½in) free at each side to allow for the seam allowance. Sew straight across the bottom of the pockets.

13 Remove all the pins. Fold the two short sides right sides together, making sure the pockets are tucked out of the way of your stitch line. Sew together to make a tube.

14 Sew in the circular base with the fleece backing. To help with fitting, fold both the tube and base into quarters and crease, then pin together at these marks before sewing. Remove the pins and turn the right side out.

15 Sew a button over the dividing stitch line between each pocket – you will have two buttons left over.

16 Fold the remaining 63.5 x 20cm (25 x 8in) piece of fabric A into a tube, aligning the short ends and with the right sides facing. Sew along the short ends, leaving a gap of about 10cm (4in) for turning. Insert the remaining circular base – right sides facing in – in the same way as in step 14. This is your lining.

17 Keeping the lining section inside out, drop the outer pocketed section inside the lining, so that the right sides are together; line up the side seams. Insert the drawstring section between the outer and lining pieces, aligning the raw edges. Sew all the way around the top.

18 Turn right side out through the gap in the lining. Sew the opening closed by hand, then push the lining inside the caddy and press. Edge stitch around the top of the bag – you may need to use the free arm on your sewing machine.

19 Thread the ribbon through your bodkin, then feed this through the drawstring channel and pull tight. Alternatively, pin a safety pin through the end of the ribbon, and use this to help guide the ribbon through.

20 Attach the handle with the ends on opposite sides of the top of the caddy using embroidery thread: take the needle from the inside of the caddy, through the handle and a button, back through the caddy and tie on the inside. Don't pull the thread too tight – the handle needs to pivot.

21 When you're not using the caddy, pull the drawstring tight and use the handle to carry. When you're using it, fold the handle over and undo the drawstring.

Cutting Mat Carrier

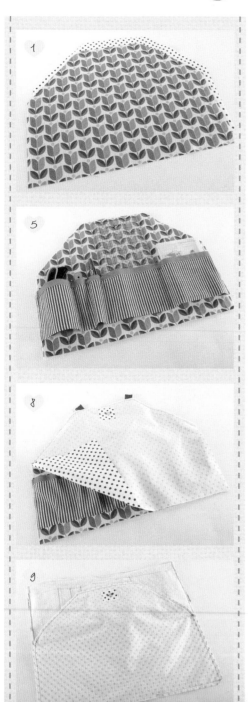

If you're going to a craft class or just need to store your cutting equipment, this pretty case can be made to any size you like.

Materials

Based on a cutting mat measuring 46 x 30cm (18 x 12in):

- 2 pieces of fabric measuring 53.5 x 40.5cm (21 x 16in)
- 2 pieces of fusible fleece measuring 53.5 x 40.5cm (21 x 16in)
- 2 pieces of lining fabric measuring 53.5 x 40.5cm (21 x 16in)
- for the 2 pockets, 4 pieces of fabric: 2 plain and 2 patterned, each measuring 63.5 x 15cm (25 x 6in)
- magnetic clasp
- 2 lengths of 2.5cm (1in) wide webbing, each measuring 40.5cm (16in)

Tools

- sewing machine and thread
- iron
- erasable fabric pen

1 Fuse the fleece to the back of the outer fabric pieces. Measure 15cm (6in) down the sides and along the top from each top corner, and cut at an angle between these points. Repeat to trim the lining pieces.

2 Fold the lining pieces in half to crease the centre lines. Measure and mark 4cm (1½in) down from the top edge. Cut two 5cm (2in) squares of lining fabric from the leftover corners, and place behind your marks – this will help to strengthen the fabric around the clasps. Apply one half of the clasp to each lining piece at the mark.

3 To make up the first pocket, place a patterned fabric piece and plain fabric piece right sides together and sew along the long edges. Turn right side out, and roll so that a 1cm (½in) strip of lining shows at the top. Press, then top-stitch along the seam.

4 Pin the raw side edges to the sides of the front of the bag, 5cm (2in) up from the base.

5 Pin the pocket at intervals to make dividing pockets – these can be any size you like. If you have specific tools you'd like to store, pop them inside the pocket and place your pins around them.

6 Mark the dividing lines with your erasable pen, then sew, removing the pins. Top-stitch the bottom of the pocket, folding the loose fabric into pleats as you sew. Sew the side seams. Repeat to create and attach another pocket to the back of the bag.

7 Tack/baste the webbing handles, facing inwards, to the top side of each half of the bag.

8 Place a lining piece over the front outer panel, right sides facing. Sew together along the top three sides, trapping the webbing handle in place. Repeat with the back panel.

9 Sew the two pocket panels right sides together, starting and stopping at the point where the lining meets. Fold the flaps out of the way, and sew the lining pieces together in the same way, leaving a gap in the base of about 15cm (6in) for turning.

10 Turn right side out and press. Sew the opening in the lining closed then push the lining inside the bag. Press around the top then edge stitch.

Sewing Circle

Keep your sewing room organised with this vintage-style pocket – the perfect place to keep pencils, threads or patterns. Try making matching circles in different sizes to create a pretty display.

Materials

- 2 circles of patterned fabric measuring 30cm (12in) across
- 2 circles of plain fabric measuring 30cm (12in) across
- 2 circles of firm wadding/batting measuring 30cm (12in) across
- 1 rectangle of contrast fabric for the pocket, measuring 19 x 25.5cm (7½ x 10in)
- 61cm (24in) of 5mm (¼in) wide ribbon for the loops
- 20cm (8in) of 2.5cm (1in) wide lace to trim the pocket
- 138cm (1½yd) of 5mm (¼in) wide ribbon for the flowers
- 15cm (6in) of 5mm (¼in) wide green ribbon for leaves
- about 20 seed beads

Tools

- sewing machine and thread
- erasable fabric pen and ruler
- fabric scissors
- large-eyed needle
- beading needle

1 Fold the top of one of the patterned circles over by 10cm (4in). Press the fold to create a crease.

2 Open out the fabric and draw a line across the crease with an erasable fabric pen. Starting in the centre, draw a row of vertical lines 4cm (1½in) apart across the entire circle. Place the circle on top of a piece of wadding/batting, then sew along the vertical lines to quilt.

3 Cut a 6.5cm (2½in) length of ribbon and sew to the top of the circle, facing inwards, 1cm (½in) each side of the centre point.

4 To make the pocket, fold the rectangle of fabric in half, right sides together, so that it measures 19 x 13cm (7½ x 5in). Sew around the three open sides, leaving a gap of about 7.5cm (3in) in the bottom edge for turning. Snip off the corners.

5 Turn right side out and press. Edge stitch across the top, then sew the lace just under these stitches, securing at each end. Take the remaining patterned circle and place on top of a circle of wadding/batting. Sew the pocket 6.5cm (2½in) down from the top, sewing around the sides and bottom, securing your turning gap as you go. Cut a 30cm (12in) length of ribbon and sew in a loop, facing inwards, to the centre top.

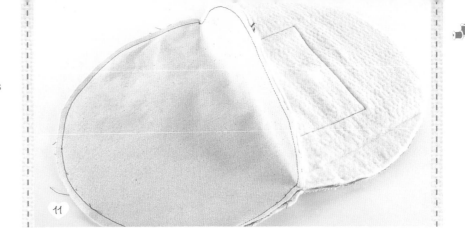

6 Take one of the plain fabric circles, fold over the top by 10cm (4in) and crease as before. This will be the flap on the front of your project. Draw three circles just to the left-hand side of the flap, measuring 4cm (1½in) across. Draw five spokes in each circle. Make sure you don't draw these circles too close to the edge of the fabric as you don't want them to disappear into the seam! Working from the centre outwards, sew a stitch along each spoke line and secure the thread.

7 Cut the long piece of ribbon into three 46cm (18in) lengths. Thread one end through the eye of your needle, and bring up through the centre of one of the circles, leaving about 2.5cm (1in) at the back. The ribbon will be quite difficult to pull through, so persevere – a thimble may help! Weave the ribbon around the five spokes – over and under – and allow it to twist. Keep it quite tight at the centre and looser around the edges.

8 When you have a full flower, take the needle back through the fabric and sew the two ends together – this is less bulky than knotting. Repeat for the other two flowers.

9 Hand sew a few seed beads to the centres and around each flower. Cut three lengths of green ribbon, 5cm (2in) in length. Fold them in half and sew behind each flower for leaves.

10 Place the fabric circles right sides together in pairs, the ribbon flowers piece with the quilted patterned piece, and the plain circle with the patterned pocket piece. Sew together around the top, starting and stopping at the crease line.

11 Sew the bottom of the embroidered plain circle to the bottom of the patterned quilted circle, starting and stopping at the crease line.

12 Sew together the patterned pocket circle with the plain circle, starting and stopping at the crease line, but leave a gap in the bottom of about 10cm (4in) for turning. Turn right side out, sew the opening closed and push the lining inside. Press, then add a little bow to the top as a finishing touch.

Tool Roll

Scissors, rotary cutter, screwdriver, embroidery hoop... this useful roll keeps your needlecraft tools organised and easy to find. You can easily adapt the sizes of the pockets to accommodate different sized tools.

Materials

- 2 pieces of coordinating fabric measuring 58.5 x 29cm (23 x 11½in)
- 2 pieces of wadding/batting measuring 58.5 x 29cm (23 x 11½in)
- 2 pieces of outer and 2 pieces of lining fabric measuring 15 x 30cm (6 x 12in) each, for the zipped pouch
- 25.5cm (10in) zip
- 94cm (37in) length of 5mm (¼in) wide ribbon
- 5cm (2in) hook and loop fastening
- 2 pieces of coordinating fabric measuring 20 x 15cm (8 x 6in), for the embroidery hoop pocket
- 2 buttons
- 2 pieces of fabric measuring 28 x 15cm (11 x 6in) for the tool pocket
- 2 pieces of fabric measuring 7.5 x 20cm (3 x 8in) for the pocket flap

Tools

- sewing machine and thread
- iron
- 10cm (4in) circle template such as a saucer
- erasable fabric pen
- repositionable spray adhesive

1 Stick the wadding/batting to the wrong side of each long piece of fabric using repositionable spray adhesive. Using your template and erasable pen, draw a curve on each corner and cut out.

2 Take the four zipped pouch fabric pieces, and cut a 4cm (1½in) square from each corner.

3 Sew the top edges of the outer fabric to either side of the zip, right sides together.

4 Sew the lining pieces to the opposite sides of the zip tape.

5 Open the fabric away from the zip and press, then top-stitch alongside the zip.

6 Trim the zip back to the fabric and, to help when constructing the pouch, hand sew the open end of the zip together. Leave the zip about halfway open. Fold the fabrics over so that the outer pieces are right sides together and so are the lining pieces. Sew around the sides, but not around the cut-out corners. Leave a 10cm (4in) gap in the long lining edge for turning.

7 Pinch each of the four cut-out corners, pull out so that the side seams meet the base seam, and sew.

8 Do the same with the corners around the zip, but this time sew across two corners together, sandwiching the zip in the centre.

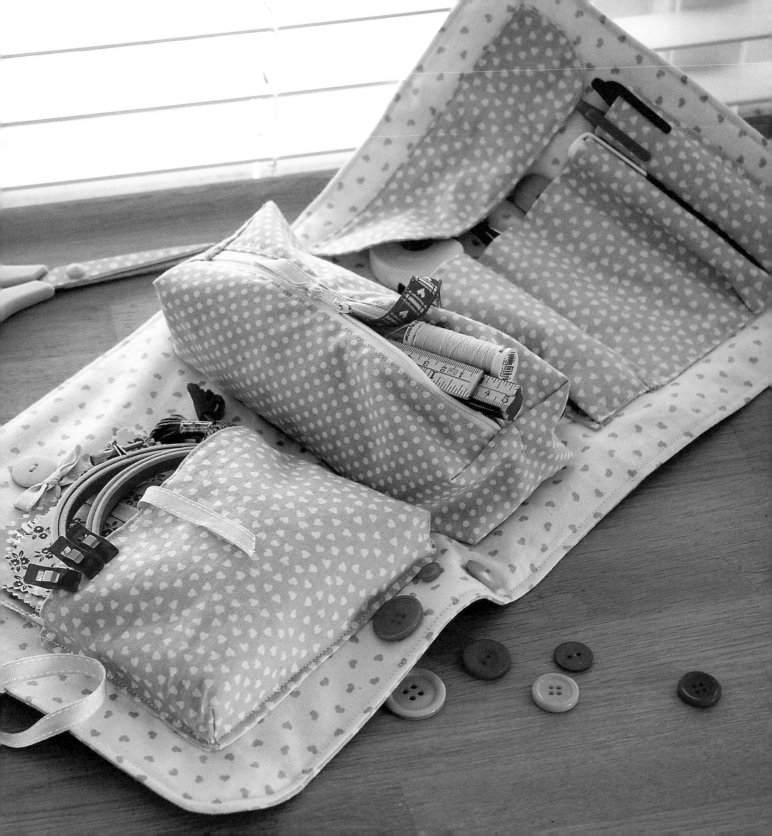

9 Turn the right side out and sew the opening closed. Push the lining inside the pouch.

10 Fold the long piece of fabric that will be the inside of the roll in half and crease to mark the centre line. Place the pouch centrally over this line, and pin on the inside. Wiggle the pouch under your sewing machine needle and sew around the base in a square. Alternatively, you could sew by hand. Remove the pins. Cut a 7.5cm (3in) length of ribbon and thread through the end of the zip slider, knot and cut the ends at an angle to stop them fraying.

11 Take the embroidery hoop pocket pieces and cut a 2.5cm (1in) square from each of the bottom corners.

12 Sew the edges of the cut-out squares together, right sides facing, as if they were darts.

13 Sew the two pieces right sides together, lining up the darts, and leaving a gap of about 7.5cm (3in) in the bottom edge for turning. Snip across the corners, turn right side out and press.

14 Edge stitch across the top of the pocket. Pin in place to the left of the zipped pouch, 5cm (2in) from the raw left-hand edge of the base fabric. Sew, then remove the pins.

15 Cut a 15cm (6in) length of ribbon, and sew one half of the hook and loop fastening to one end. Sew the other end centrally, 9cm (3½in) above the pocket. Cover the end with a button, and decorate with a bow cut from 7.5cm (3in) of ribbon if you wish.

16 Sew the second half of the hook and loop fastening to the front of the pocket, centrally, 6.5cm (2½in) from the top.

17 To make the tool pocket, sew the two pieces of fabric right sides together, leaving a gap in one side of about 7.5cm (3in) for turning. Snip across the corners, then turn through the gap and press. Edge stitch across the top.

18 Sew the sides of the pocket to the right-hand side of the roll, 3cm (1¼in) from the raw edge and 3cm (1¼in) from the zipped pouch. Slip the tools you wish to store inside, and pin in between them to divide into pockets.

19 Remove your tools, sew along the pinned dividing lines, then straight across the bottom of the pocket. Remove the pins.

20 Pin the two flap pieces right sides together and use your template to mark curves on the lower corners. Trim off the excess fabric then sew all round, leaving a gap in the top edge of about 7.5cm (3in). Snip off the corners and turn right side out; press. Edge stitch around the curved sides.

21 Sew along the top edge of the flap 7.5cm (3in) above the tool pockets – the flap stops your tools from falling out.

22 Cut two 20cm (8in) lengths of ribbon, and sew one piece, facing inwards, to the centre of the left-hand side of the roll.

23 Place this whole pocketed section right sides together with the remaining roll fabric, and sew all the way round, leaving a gap in one side of about 13cm (5in). Snip around the curves. Turn right side out and press. Edge stitch all the way round, sewing over the opening to close it.

24 Place your tools inside the roll, then fold over and mark the position of the second 20cm (8in) length of ribbon. Hand sew in place, then cover with a button and bow to decorate (as shown below).

Chair Storage

These handy pockets sit over the arm of your chair to help keep you organised when you're doing a bit of hand sewing – the rose pincushion adds a touch of elegance. Add more pockets if you need them, and use colours to match the decor of your room.

Materials

- 2 rectangles of fabric measuring 56 x 25.5cm (22 x 10in)
- 1 piece of the same fabric measuring 25.5cm (10in) square
- 1 piece of fusible fleece measuring 56 x 25.5cm (22 x 10in)
- 4 pieces of contrast fabric for the pockets measuring 25.5 x 13cm (10 x 5in)
- 2 25.5cm (10in) lengths of 2.5cm (1in) wide bias binding for the pocket tops
- 10 circles of patterned fabric measuring 13cm (5in) across, in four contrasting colours: I used a plain pink for the centre
- 2 circles of green fabric measuring 13cm (5in) across for the leaves
- 2m (2yds) of 2.5cm (1in) wide bias binding
- a handful of toy filling

Tools

- sewing machine and thread
- scissors
- fabric marker pen
- hand sewing needle and thread
- repositionable spray adhesive
- iron

1 Take the plain pink circle of fabric and hand sew running stitch around the edge. Push a little toy filling into the centre – on to the wrong side of the fabric – before pulling up the thread to gather, making a ball shape.

2 Mark the centre of another circle of fabric and sew the ball on top of this mark by hand. Fold the remaining patterned fabric circles in half, wrong sides together, and sew, leaving a gap of about 5cm (2in) in the curve for stuffing. Push a little toy filling into the middle, avoiding the points of the semicircles. You should have eight of these.

3 Place one of the semicircles over the ball-shaped piece, covering about a third of the dome and pin. Pin on two more semicircles in the same way, overlapping each one. Sew in place on your machine. Don't worry about the edges looking untidy – these will be covered.

4 Pin the remaining five semicircles around the edge of the first three, then sew in place.

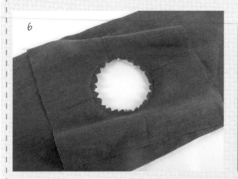

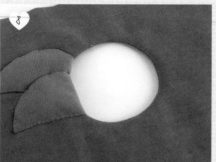

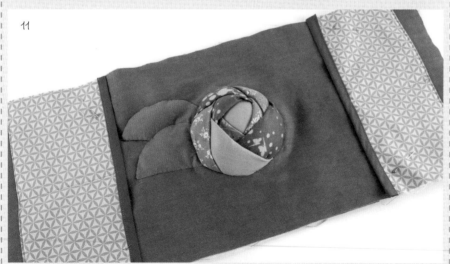

5 Mark the centre of the 25.5cm (10in) square piece of fabric on the wrong side, then draw a circle directly over this spot, 10cm (4in) across.

6 Fuse the fleece to the back of one of the large rectangular pieces of fabric. Mark the centre. Place the 25.5cm (10in) square right sides together over the centre point, and sew around the circle you've drawn. Cut around the inside of the circle through all layers of fabric, then snip the edges to help the seam sit flat. Turn right side out and press.

7 To make the leaves, fold the green fabric circles in half, right sides together, and sew from one point to about 5cm (2in) from the bottom. Turn right side out and press. Pop a little toy filling into the point of the leaves.

8 Place the leaves, overlapping slightly, to one side of the circular hole (as shown). Fold the ends inside the hole, and hand stitch in place.

9 Now push your rose pincushion into the hole from the back and pin, before hand sewing around the edge.

10 To make up the pockets, sew two pieces of pocket fabric right sides together across one long side (the bottom edges), then turn right side out and press. Apply bias tape across the top raw edge. Repeat for the second pocket.

11 Pin one pocket to each end of the long piece of fabric, 4cm (1½in) from each end, and sew across the bottom of the pockets. Fold the pockets in half to crease the centre, then top-stitch along this line to create a divider in each pocket. You can make as many pockets as you like!

12 Spray the back with repositionable adhesive, and place on top of the remaining rectangle of fabric, with wrong sides facing. Sew bias tape around the edge to finish.

Tip

After making the rose to step 4, you could make a little extra pincushion. Sew bias tape around the edge of the circle but before folding the tape over, glue an old CD to the base, covered with another 13cm (5in) circle of fabric. Fold over the tape and either hand sew or glue in place. I've decorated this one with lace trim, a button and beads, which gives it a vintage feel.

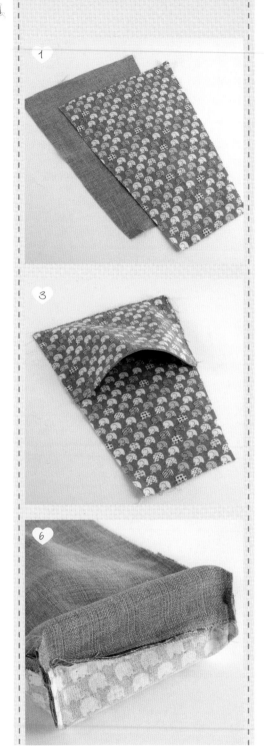

Seam Press

I've designed this pressing tool with a pocket on the back to protect my fingers, a square top that is perfect for pressing the inside of bags, and a narrow end for smaller seams. It's packed with sawdust to absorb any steam. It's a handy tool for pressing projects that have dimension, like bags, where you don't want to flatten the item when ironing.

Materials

I've used a linen-mix fabric, which is slightly heavier than craft cotton.

♥ 1 rectangle of patterned fabric measuring 23 x 33cm (9 x 13in)
♥ 1 rectangle of contrast plain fabric measuring 23 x 33cm (9 x 13in)
♥ 1 rectangle of patterned fabric measuring 23 x 18cm (9 x 7in)
♥ 1 rectangle of contrast plain fabric measuring 23 x 18cm (9 x 7in)
♥ sawdust

Tools

♥ sewing machine and thread
♥ scissors
♥ fabric marker pen
♥ hand-sewing needle and thread
♥ iron

1 Measure 5cm (2in) in from the bottom of each large piece of fabric and trim from this mark to the top corners.

2 To make the mitt section, take the remaining two pieces of fabric and sew right sides together across the bottom edge. Turn over to the right side and press, then edge stitch across the seam for a neat finish.

3 Place this pocket over the top of the patterned rectangle and line up the sides before sewing together close to the edge – you'll notice the pocket side is wider at the base so creates an arc.

4 Place the remaining rectangle of fabric right sides together with the pocketed side, and sew around all sides leaving a gap in the bottom edge of 7.5cm (3in) for stuffing.

5 Pinch the two top corners so that the top seam sits on top of the side seams and pin. Mark lines across these seams, 4cm (1½in) from the points. Sew along the lines.

6 Cut off the excess fabric from the corners – this will make the top square.

7 Turn right side out through the gap in the bottom, then stuff tightly with sawdust. Pack the sawdust into the opening until you just can't fit in any more!

8 Hand sew the opening closed with an over edge stitch.

Ironing Station

For ironing small pieces of fabric, I find this converted TV table the perfect pressing station! I keep mine at the side of my sewing table – the handy detachable pouch (see page 48) stores my mini iron.

Materials

- 1 foldaway TV table: the top of mine measures 48 x 38cm (19 x 15in)
- 48 x 38cm (19 x 15in) table protector
- 48 x 38cm (19 x 15in) heat-resistant batting/wadding
- 58 x 48cm (23 x 19in) reflective ironing board cover fabric
- 58 x 48cm (23 x 19in) cover fabric
- 210cm (84in) of 1cm (½in) wide ribbon
- 1.5m (60in) of 5mm (¼in) wide elastic
- 2 buttons, one smaller than the other
- 10cm (4in) of hook and loop fastening

Tools

- sewing machine and thread
- repositionable spray adhesive
- scissors
- staple gun (or a small tack and hammer)

1 Turn your table upside down on top of the table protector and draw around the outline before cutting to shape. Use this as a template to cut the same shape from the wadding/batting. Cut the cover fabric and ironing board fabric 5cm (2in) larger all round.

2 Spray the top of the table with a little adhesive, and pop on the protector, then spray again and lay the batting on top.

3 Cut the ribbon into twenty-eight 7.5cm (3in) strips. Fold in half to make tabs, and pin evenly around the cover, with the folded edge facing inwards. Make sure there is a tab over each corner. Sew close to the edge to hold in place. Remove the pins.

4 Place the reflective fabric on top of the cover fabric, right sides together, pin, then sew all the way round, leaving a gap of about 13cm (5in) in one side for turning.

5 Remove the pins and turn the right side out. Press, then edge stitch all the way around – this will close the opening.

6 Thread the elastic through the ribbon tabs and knot. Fit over the table top. If needed, you can pull the elastic tighter and re-knot.

7 Sew the smaller button onto the larger one. I like to sew them together before sewing to my projects – it makes it easier to find the holes with the needle when they're already lined up! Sew the buttons to one side of the cover, about 10cm (4in) from a corner.

8 Staple the hook and loop fastening to the underside of the table, 7.5cm (3in) from the position of the button.

Mini-iron Pouch

This little pouch is 20 x 13cm (8 x 5in) – ideal for a mini-iron. You could also use it to hold other items such as a small water spray bottle.

Materials

- 2 pieces of fabric measuring 13 x 23cm (5 x 9in)
- 2 pieces of heat-resistant batting/ wadding measuring 13 x 23cm (5 x 9in)
- 2 pieces of reflective ironing board fabric measuring 13 x 23cm (5 x 9in)
- 2 buttons, one smaller than the other
- elastic hair band

Tools

- sewing machine and thread
- rotary cutter and mat
- scissors
- repositionable spray adhesive
- hand-sewing needle and thread

1 Adhere the wadding/batting to the wrong side of the outer fabric using spray adhesive. Cut a 2.5cm (1in) square from the two bottom corners of all pieces.

2 Place a reflective lining piece over each fabric piece, right sides facing, and sew the top short edge seam. Open out the pieces as shown.

3 Now place these pieces right sides together, matching fabric to fabric and lining to lining. Sew along each side, omitting the cut-out corners, and leaving a gap of 5cm (2in) in the bottom of the lining for turning.

4 Pinch the cut-out squares so that the bottom and side seams meet, and sew across the openings. This will shape the base of the pouch.

5 Turn the pouch right side out and hand sew the opening closed. Push the lining inside the bag and press, then edge stitch around the top.

6 Sew the smaller button to the larger one then sew to the centre top of the back of the pouch. Loop the hair elastic around the button.

7 Your pouch can now hang from the side of your new ironing table! Pop your mini iron into the pouch – the hook and loop fastening will keep your cable tidy.

Sewing Machine Cover

When your machine is not in use it's advisable to keep it dust-free; many machines will come with an unattractive plastic sheath. My dust cover not only looks stylish, but is practical too, with its hole in the top so that you can access the handle, and large pocket on the back for your extension table. If you don't have one, you could store patterns in here instead.

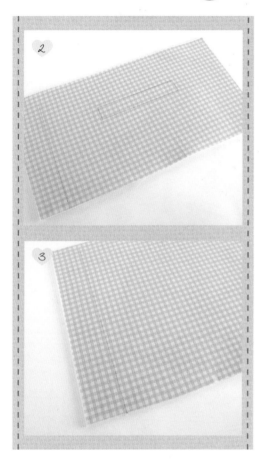

Materials

My measurements are based on my machine, which measures 39.5 x 28 x 20cm (15½ x 11 x 8in). Measure the dimensions of your machine first and adjust if necessary – you'll notice that the fabric pieces are 2.5cm (1in) taller and wider.

- ♥ 2 pieces of outer fabric measuring 42 x 30cm (16½ x 12in), for the sides
- ♥ 2 pieces of lining measuring 42 x 30cm (16½ x 12in)
- ♥ 2 pieces of single-sided fusible foam stabiliser measuring 42 x 30cm (16½ x 12in)
- ♥ 2 pieces of outer fabric measuring 23 x 30cm (9 x 12in)
- ♥ 2 pieces of lining fabric measuring 23 x 30cm (9 x 12in)
- ♥ 2 pieces of single-sided fusible foam stabiliser measuring 23 x 30cm (9 x 12in)
- ♥ 1 piece of outer fabric measuring 40.5 x 23cm (16 x 9in), for the top
- ♥ 1 piece of lining fabric measuring 40.5 x 23cm (16 x 9in)
- ♥ 1 piece of single-sided fusible foam stabiliser measuring 40.5 x 23cm (16 x 9in)
- ♥ 2 pieces of fabric measuring 45.5 x 25.5cm (18 x 10in) for the pocket
- ♥ 1 piece of wadding/batting measuring 45.5 x 25.5cm (18 x 10in)
- ♥ around 30 6.5cm (2½in) squares of patterned fabric for the patchwork: I used a charm pack and cut the pieces into four
- ♥ 1.2m (47in) of 1cm (½in) wide lace
- ♥ 80cm (31in) of 5mm (¼in) wide lace
- ♥ 10 buttons
- ♥ 1.8m (70in) of 2.5cm (1in) wide bias tape

Tools

- ♥ sewing machine and thread
- ♥ iron
- ♥ erasable fabric pen

1 Fuse a piece of foam to the wrong side of each piece of outer fabric.

2 Measure on your machine the position of the handle, as it's not always in the centre, and transfer this mark to the top piece of fabric, forming a box shape that your handle will fit through. Mine measures 2.5 x 15cm (1 x 6in). Draw a vertical line 4cm (1½in) from the left-hand edge with your erasable fabric pen.

3 Draw a vertical line 4cm (1½in) from the left-hand side of the front of the cover, and another 4cm (1½in) from the right-hand side of the back of the cover.

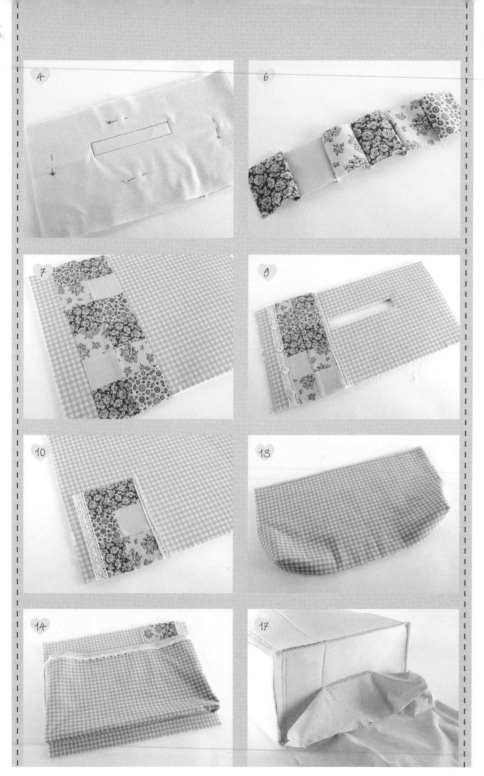

4 Transfer the box shape for the handle to the top section of lining fabric, and pin right sides together with the outer top fabric. Sew around the box.

5 Cut straight down the centre of the box and into the corners, being careful not to cut into the stitches! Turn right side out by pushing the lining through the hole; press.

6 Sew together six of the patchwork squares, right sides facing, to create a strip.

7 Join another six pieces in the same way, press, then sew the two strips together along a long edge. Press again. Place over the front of the cover, aligning the patchwork strip with the drawn line.

8 Sew a strip of 1cm (½in) wide lace ribbon to the left-hand side to cover the raw edge of the patchwork, and a 5mm (¼in) strip to the right. Trim away any excess fabric and lace, then add six buttons evenly to the wider strip of lace.

9 Repeat steps 6–8 for the top section of the cover, using ten patches, the two strips of lace ribbon and four buttons.

10 It's not necessary to take the patchwork all the way down the back of the cover, as it will be partially covered by the pocket. Use six patches and the lace ribbon – do not worry about the buttons. Take the pieces halfway down and turn under the ends to make neat.

11 Fuse the wadding/batting to the wrong side of the outer pocket piece. Cut a 2.5cm (1in) square from each bottom corner of both pocket pieces.

12 For both the lining and outer pocket pieces, pinch the edges of the cut-out squares together and sew to make the box shape of the base.

13 Sew the outer pocket piece right sides together with the pocket lining across the bottom edge. Fold over so that the wrong sides are together, then apply a strip of bias tape across the top.

14 Sew a strip of lace just under the bias tape on the pocket front. Pin the pocket to the back of the cover, 4cm (1½in) up from the bottom, with the raw edges meeting at the side. Top-stitch the bottom and sides in place then remove your pins.

15 Sew the four outer side pieces together, right sides facing, to form a tube. Trim away the foam stabiliser to the seam and turn right side out. Top-stitch along the seams – this will help to keep the cover square.

16 Turn the outer cover inside out again, and sew in the top section, matching up the corners and making sure the lining is out of the way as you sew.

17 Sew the remaining four lining pieces together, right sides facing, to make a tube. Sew the tube of lining to the top of the lining in the same way.

18 Turn the cover right side out and push the lining inside. Match up the raw edges and sew, before applying bias binding around the bottom edge. To help keep the lining in place, sew a few hand stitches in the top corners through all layers.

The front of the cover.

The back of the cover.

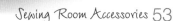

Pin and Pattern Pouch ♡

Pop this pocket at the end of your sewing table to keep lightweight items such as your pins and patterns in place!

Materials

- ♥ 2 pieces of fabric measuring 30 x 46cm (12 x 18in)
- ♥ 2 pieces of fabric measuring 28 x 39.5cm (11 x 15½in) for the pocket
- ♥ a strip of packing tape 38cm (15in) long – trim it to 5mm (¼in) wide
- ♥ 1 piece of fusible interfacing measuring 30 x 46cm (12 x 18in)
- ♥ 1 piece of fusible interfacing measuring 28 x 39.5cm (11 x 15½in), for the pocket
- ♥ 2 cups of dry white sand
- ♥ 2m (2yds) of 2.5cm (1in) bias tape

Tools

- ♥ sewing machine and thread
- ♥ fabric scissors
- ♥ hand-sewing needle and thread
- ♥ 15cm (6in) round template – I used a plate
- ♥ fabric marker pen
- ♥ repositionable spray adhesive
- ♥ iron

1   Fuse the interfacing to the wrong side of the outer pocket fabric. Mark then cut a 5cm (2in) square from the bottom two corners of both pieces of pocket fabric.

2   On both the outer and lining pocket pieces, fold the cut corner sections together, right sides facing, and sew to make the box shape of the bottom of the pocket. Place the outer and lining pieces together, right sides facing, and sew across the top to join them. Open them out and re-fold so that the wrong sides are now facing. Top-stitch around the bottom and sides.

3   Sew a strip of bias tape across the top of the pocket, then feed the packing tape through it – cut the tape 1cm (½in) shorter so that you don't sew over it at the seams.

4   Iron the fusible interfacing to the wrong side of the large piece of fabric – this not only helps it to keep its shape, it also stops the sand coming through the weave of the fabric.

5   Spray the back of the remaining piece of fabric with the glue, and position on top of the back of the large piece of fabric – on top of the interfacing.

6   Draw around the bottom two corners of your large fabric piece using the 15cm (6in) round template, and cut the curves.

9

10

7 Fold over the top edge of the large fabric piece by about 10cm (4in), turn under the raw edge and top-stitch in place. Make a 'pouch' for the sand by sewing down the right-hand edge of this tube.

8 Pin the pocket to the front of the large fabric piece, making sure it's central, and sew close to the edge around the sides and bottom edge to attach.

9 Pour the sand into the pouch until it is firmly filled, and hand sew the opening closed with tiny overedge stitches. Don't attempt to use your sewing machine – the sand will spill into it!

10 Attach the bias tape all the way around the raw edges, make sure that the areas over the sand pocket are sewn by hand.

Tip

If your packing tape has been folded it won't curve perfectly, so warm it with a hairdryer to soften it, then mould it into a curved shape.

Sewing Book Cover

Many of us like to keep notes about our projects, favourite fabric shops, measurements, or hints and tips we've picked up on our sewing journey. This simple notebook cover can easily be personalised with an embroidered name on the cover.

Materials

My measurements are for an A5 notebook: 15 x 21.75cm (6 x 8½in)

- ❤ 2 rectangles of fabric measuring 48 x 25.5cm (19 x 10in)
- ❤ 1 piece of single-sided fusible fleece measuring 48 x 25.5cm (19 x 10in)
- ❤ 5.75 x 10cm (2¼ x 4in) piece of co-ordinating fabric for the mannequin appliqué
- ❤ 7.5 x 16.5cm (3 x 6½in) contrasting fabric for the pen pocket
- ❤ 4 buttons: I like to sew 2 buttons of different sizes together
- ❤ 2 strips of bias-cut fabric measuring 46cm (18in) long by 5cm (2in) wide, for binding
- ❤ 76cm (30in) of 1cm (½in) wide ribbon
- ❤ 5cm (2in) length of pearl beading

Tools

- ❤ sewing machine, thread and free-motion foot
- ❤ hand-sewing needle and thread
- ❤ erasable fabric pen
- ❤ repositionable spray adhesive
- ❤ 2.5cm (1in) bias binding tool
- ❤ fabric clips

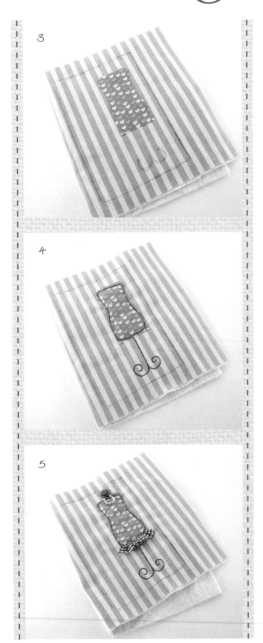

1 Fuse the fleece to the wrong side of the outer rectangle of fabric. Wrap the fabric around your diary or notebook and mark the edges of the book on the right side of the fabric with an erasable fabric pen – this is to outline the area you can decorate.

2 To make the mannequin shape, fold the piece of fabric in half lengthways and cut a curve just above halfway on the long side to make a 'waist'. Curve the top corners to create 'shoulders'.

3 Spray the wrong side of the mannequin shape with adhesive, and position on the cover, 2.5cm (1in) from the top right-hand corner of your drawn area. Draw a stand with two curly feet from the base of the mannequin with your erasable pen.

4 Put the free-motion embroidery foot on to your sewing machine and embroider three or four times around the outline. If you don't have the free-motion foot you could use a satin stitch instead.

5 Cut a 15cm (6in) length of ribbon. Sew along one edge with running stitch and pull to gather the ribbon to 5cm (2in) in length. Hand sew it in place across the bottom of the mannequin. Sew the pearl beads to the neck of the mannequin. Sew a small button on top of a larger one then attach over the ends of the beads.

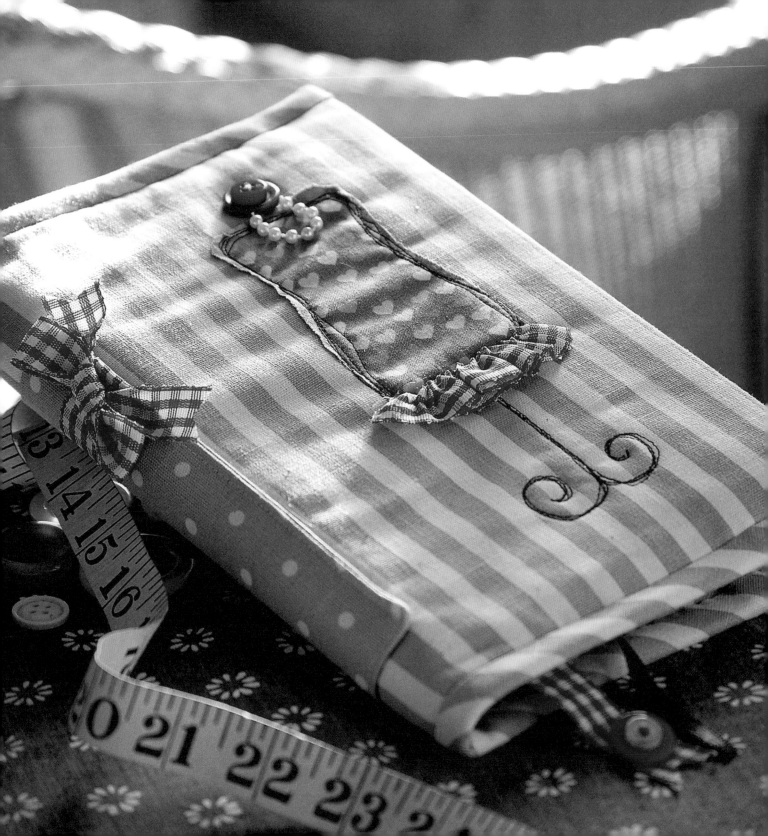

6 Cut a 35.5cm (14in) length of ribbon and tack/baste to the centre top of the cover, facing inwards. Sew two more buttons to the other end as before.

7 To make the pen pocket, fold the strip of fabric in half lengthways, right sides together. Sew along the three raw edges leaving a small gap of about 4cm (1½in) in the bottom for turning. Snip across the corners, then turn right side out and press. Wrap a piece of ribbon measuring 9cm (3½in) around the pocket piece about 2.5cm (1in) down from the top and hand sew to the reverse.

8 Pin the pocket to the spine of the cover, 6.5cm (2½in) from the top. Top-stitch along the bottom edge and two sides. Use the remaining ribbon to make a bow – sew this to the side of the pocket.

9 Sew the outer and lining fabrics right sides together, along the short sides. Turn right way out and press. Top-stitch along the seams.

10 To make the bias binding, use your 2.5cm (1in) bias binding tool and iron the sides of each strip to the centre. For this project it's not necessary to cut the fabric on the bias as it won't be sewn around a curve, but bias cutting a striped fabric gives an interesting chevron effect.

11 Fold over each short sewn end of the cover by 4cm (1½in) – as the fabric is quite thick, it may be easier to clip than pin at this stage. Sew the bias tape across each long side, right sides together, leaving it about 1cm (½in) longer than the cover at each end.

12 Fold the tape over the raw edge, tuck the ends inwards to make neat and hand sew with a slip stitch. Slip your notebook inside the sleeve and you're finished!

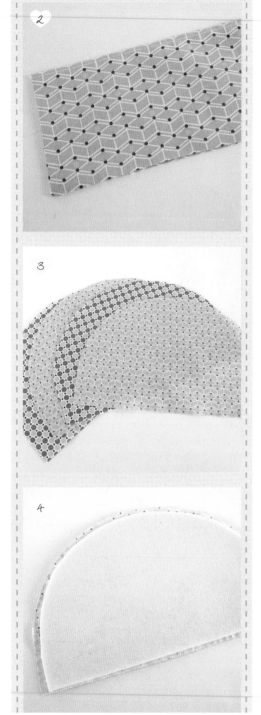

Carry Case

If you're off to a workshop or just want to keep your sewing area tidy, this useful case will hold anything from fat quarters to patterns. It would also make a lovely vanity case!

Materials

- 2 rectangles of outer fabric measuring 30 x 20cm (12 x 8in)
- 2 pieces of lining fabric measuring 30 x 20cm (12 x 8in)
- 2 pieces of foam stabiliser measuring 30 x 20cm (12 x 8in)
- for the zipped panel, one strip of outer fabric measuring 58.5 x 4cm (23 x 1½in)
- 1 strip of lining fabric measuring 58.5 x 4cm (23 x 1½in)
- 1 strip of foam stabiliser measuring 57 x 2.5cm (22½ x 1in)
- 1 strip of outer fabric measuring 58.5 x 9cm (23 x 3½in)
- 1 strip of lining fabric measuring 58.5 x 9cm (23 x 3½in)
- 1 strip of foam stabiliser measuring 57 x 7cm (22½ x 2¾in)
- for the back panel, 1 rectangle of outer fabric measuring 30 x 13cm (12 x 5in)
- 1 piece of lining fabric measuring 30 x 13cm (12 x 5in)
- 1 piece of foam stabiliser measuring 29 x 11.5cm (11½ x 4½in)
- for the pocket, 1 piece of fabric measuring 18 x 15cm (7 x 6in)
- for the handle, 1 piece of fabric measuring 6.5 x 23cm (2½ x 9in)
- 1 strip of foam stabiliser measuring 2 x 20cm (¾ x 8in)
- 61cm (24in) zip – I've used a continuous zip with two sliders that meet in the middle
- 30cm (12in) circle template

Tools

- sewing machine and thread
- iron
- repositionable spray adhesive
- fabric clips

1 First, make up the pocket by folding the fabric in half along the shorter side, right sides together. Sew around the raw edges, leaving a gap in the long side of about 7.5cm (3in) for turning. Snip off the corners.

2 Turn right side out and press. Edge stitch across the folded side.

3 Take the 30 x 20cm (12 x 8in) rectangles of outer and lining fabrics and the foam stabiliser, and, using your 30cm (12in) circle template, draw then cut a curve to one side of each piece.

4 Trim away 5mm (¼in) from the edges of the foam stabiliser pieces to leave a seam allowance around the fabric pieces. Use a little repositionable spray adhesive to adhere the foam stabiliser to the wrong sides of the outer fabrics.

5 To make the handle, wrap the fabric around its corresponding foam stabiliser, folding in the raw edges. Edge stitch all the way round.

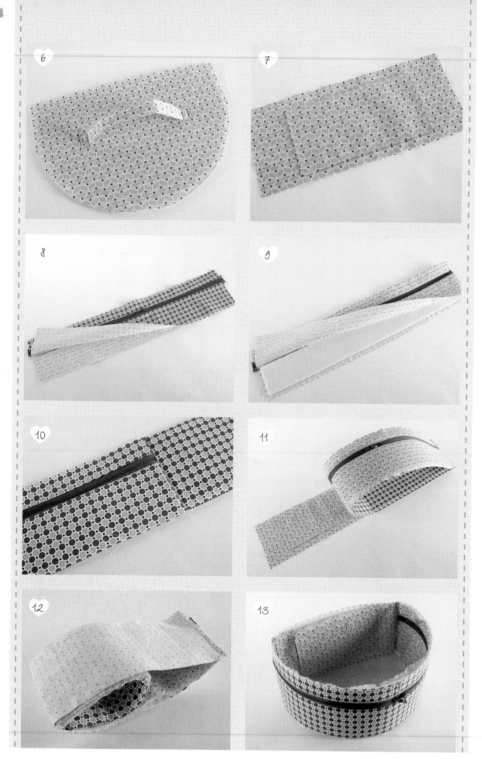

6 Measure and mark 7.5cm (3in) from the straight side of the lid (one of your backed outer pieces created in step 4), and 7.5cm (3in) from the curved side – sew the handle in place in a box shape.

7 Sew the sides and bottom of the pocket, centrally to the back lining piece of fabric.

8 Sew the top and bottom outer zip panel pieces to either side of the zip tape, right sides together. Then sew the linings to the opposite sides. Press, then top-stitch along the seam.

9 Spray one side of the zip-panel foam stabiliser pieces with repositionable adhesive and adhere them to the outer fabric, either side of the zip.

10 Spray and adhere the foam stabiliser to the outer back panel. Sew the outer back panel to the zip section right sides together along one short end. Then sew the back lining to the same seam, right side facing the lining side of the zip panel. Press, then top-stitch.

11 Fold the zipped section over so that the opposite ends meet, and sew the outer pieces right sides together.

12 This next bit may seem a bit tricky – fold the lining pieces right sides together, rolling the zipped section out of the way; sew.

13 Open out this section and you'll see the shape of the case forming. Top-stitch along the remaining seam.

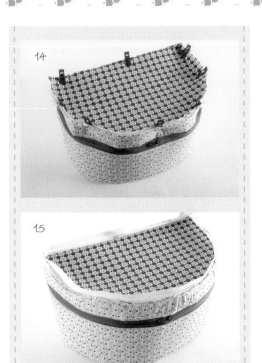

14 Turn this ring inside out. Use the adhesive spray to secure the lining to the lid and base pieces from step 4, wrong sides together. Clip the top of the case to the sides, with right sides together (this may now be too thick to pin).

15 Sew all the way round and remove the clips as you go. Apply bias tape all the way round, folding the end inwards as you start and overlapping by about 1cm (½in) when the two ends meet.

16 Fold the tape over and hand sew with a slip stitch. Repeat at the base of the case.

17 Turn the case right side out and press. Your seam press made on page 44 will come in handy here!

18 Fill with fabrics, scissors and threads and off you go!